Lace
Its Origin
and History

Samuel L. Goldenberg

Brentano's
New York
1904

Copyrighted, 1904,
BY
Samuel L. Goldenberg.

Barbara Uttmann, A. D. 1561.

"I have here only a nosegay of culled flowers. and have brought nothing of my own but the thread that ties them together."—*Montaigne*.

THE task of the author of this work has not been an attempt to brush the dust of ages from the early history of lace in the hope of contributing to the world's store of knowledge on the subject. His purpose, rather, has been to present to those whose relation to lace is primarily a commercial one a compendium that may, perchance, in times of doubt, serve as a practical guide.

Though this plan has been adhered to as closely as possible, the history of lace is so interwoven with life's comedies and tragedies, extending back over five centuries, that there must be, here and there in the following pages, a reminiscent tinge of this association.

Lace is, in fact, so indelibly associated with the chalets perched high on mountain tops, with little cottages in the valleys of the Appenines and Pyrenees, with sequestered convents in provincial France, with the raiment of men and women whose names loom large in the history of the world, and the futile as well as the successful efforts of inventors to relieve tired eyes and weary fingers, that, no matter how one attempts to treat the subject, it must be colored now and again with the hues of many peoples of many periods.

The author, in avowing his purpose to give this work a practical cast, does not wish to be understood as minimizing the importance of any of the standard works compiled by those whose years of study and research among ancient volumes and musty manuscripts in many tongues have been a labor of love. Rather would he pay the meed of tribute to those who have preserved to posterity the facts bearing upon the early history of lace, which have been garnered with such great care.

Nevertheless, most of these works, necessarily voluminous and replete with detail, are more for the connoisseur or dilettante than for the busy man of affairs upon whom the practical aspect of lace, quite dissociated from the romance in which it is steeped, always forces itself.

It is for men of this type, and with no little misgiving, and a full appreciation of how far short of his ideal the volume must be, that the author has undertaken the compilation of this work.

SAMUEL L. GOLDENBERG.

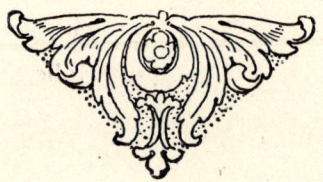

LACE:
Its Origin and History.

WHEN, where and how lace had its origin no one will pretend to say. There is a general agreement, however, that lace, as the term is understood to-day, is a comparatively modern product, it being impossible to identify any of the antique specimens preserved from the ravages of time as belonging to a period further back than the early part of the sixteenth century.

True it is that there are specimens of woven fabrics of a lacelike character which were undoubtedly made at an earlier date, but most of the authorities who have delved deep into the subject are of opinion that lace probably does not antedate A. D. 1500.

A perusal of the available records in many tongues fails to make clear just where lace was first made. Spain, Italy, Belgium, France and Germany have all claimed the honor, and each has been able to present a great deal of testimony in support of its contention; but the records of early times are so meagre and indefinite that it is impossible to bestow the coveted honor for the discovery of the art upon any one nation.

The instrument that is responsible for lace is the needle, but the earliest forms of lace were not the woven fabric that we know to-day, but rather cutwork, which, as far as we have any authentic records, was first practiced by the nuns in the convents of central and southern Europe. This work was sometimes characterized as nun's work, and was designed almost exclusively for altar decorations and the robes of prelates, thought it was also regarded as the insignia of rank and station. Some of the specimens of this work, still preserved in museums, show that the early workers possessed a skill in the art never excelled. Of course, with the progress of time, designs have become more ornate and intricate, but many of the old patterns still survive, and doubtless will continue to survive, till the end of recorded time.

The desire to elaborate the edges of plain fabrics, whether of linen or heavier material, was an entirely natural impulse to get away from the harsh simplicity of the times. To this desire must be ascribed the beginning of the mammoth lace industry of to-day.

One authority says that coeval with these styles of decoration was drawnwork, in which the weft and warp threads of plain linen were drawn out, thus forming a square of network made secure by a stitch at each intersection. The design was afterward embroidered, frequently with colors.

Perhaps, all things considered, the lace industry received its greatest impetus during the period known in history as the Renaissance, when Europe, emerging from the severe and formal garb of the Medieval Age, began to bedeck itself in the most graceful and beautiful manner.

A number of methods were employed in the production of the lace of that brilliant period, the simplest of which consisted of forming the design independently of the foundation. Threads spreading at even distances from a common center served as a framework for others which were united in squares, triangles, rosettes and other figures

Real Flemish Point.

Real Point de Venise.

worked over with the buttonhole stitch, forming in some portions open-work, in others solid embroidery. This was, in fact, the first needle-made lace, and doubtless its origin is due to the Venetians.

Through constant practice the art was developed to a very high state by the nuns, who taught their methods to the pupils of the convents, through whom the knowledge passed to the peasantry, and thus became an important industry. Perhaps, however, the development of the lace industry at this period was due more to the spread of the methods by which it was done—through books more than in any other manner—for it must be remembered that contemporaneously with the development of the industry the art of printing was in its first bloom.

As one traces the growth of lacemaking from the earliest times he is impressed with the sharp advance made at the beginning of the seventeenth century, when laceworkers, having practically exhausted the designs possible by the then known methods, invented passementerie, which were known as passements. These, speaking broadly, much resemble the passementerie of to-day.

They were made of stout linen thread in imitation of high relief work of the needle point, a thick thread being introduced to mark the salient points of the pattern. Thus the term guipure was applied to the thread lace with guipure reliefs, and the designation has since remained to all laces without grounds, in which the patterns are united by brides.

In the beginning lace was made by two entirely distinct processes, in commenting upon which we can do no better than to quote the words of Cole, which are particularly lucid and concise. He says: "It is remarkable that lacemaking should have sprung up or been invented at about the same period of time by two entirely distinct processes without relationship or evolution between them, and that the people of the countries wherein either of the inventions was made were not only unknown to each other, but apparently neither had any knowledge of the processes of lacemaking employed in the other country."

One of these processes is the employment of the needle and the single thread, wherein the work was perfected mesh by mesh, each mesh being completed as the work progressed.

The other process was by the use of many threads at once, each one attached to bobbins, for the purpose only of separating them, the meshes being made by twisting the threads a greater or less number of times. When each mesh is only partially completed the thread is carried on to the next, and so on, from side to side, the entire width of the fabric.

Felkin, in his history of embroidery and lace, says that when pillow lace was invented—about the middle of the sixteenth century—the various kinds of point lace then in use had reached a high state of perfection. Some early writers after much laborious investigation assert that pillow lace was first made in Flanders. In later years it has been almost universally attributed to Barbara, wife of Christopher Uttman; she was then dwelling with her husband at the Castle of St. Annaburg, Belgium, 1561. From the castle, where she taught the peasantry as in a school, it soon spread over the country, and women and girls of the district, finding that the making of lace was more profitable than their former employment of embroidering veils according to the Italian practice, adopted the Uttman method. No trace of this mode of making lace (by use of pillow and bobbins) can be found before this date; hence the presumption that these were the time and place of the invention of bobbin lace. Barbara Uttman died in 1575. That she was the true inventress is recorded on her tomb.

It will be seen from the foregoing that one process had its origin in Italy, and the other its origin in Belgium, though, if we accept Felkin's statement, we must accord to Italy the first honor, for he says distinctly that the Belgian peasantry gave up making lace according to the Italian method to adopt the process invented by Barbara Uttman; consequently, the Italian method must have been first. The present writer disclaims any intention to dispose of this moot question, and is only led to the above observation by reason of the high standing which Felkin's work has attained.

There are two broad divisions of lace—namely, hand-made lace and machine-made lace. In the world of commerce to-day the latter-named product, which is but a child of the former, is vastly the more important. This for the reason that hand-made lace, which is produced with such arduous toil, skill and patience, is beyond the purse of the million, and is and ever must be considered as one of the luxuries.

True, some of the simpler forms of hand-made lace are produced with relatively great facility, and the price is correspondingly cheap, as compared with the delicate, finely wrought designs, that it sometimes takes years to produce. Nor is this the sole reason for the popularity of machine-made laces, for to such perfection has the mechanical art of lacemaking attained that it is practically impossible, even for experts, to detect the difference between lace made by the deft, cunning fingers of lady or maid from the lace made possible by modern machinery.

In hand-made lace the two principal classes are the needle-point and bobbin, or pillow-made, lace. Needle-point lace is worked upon loose threads laid upon a previously drawn pattern, but which have no point of contact with one another and no coherency until the needle-work binds them together. This work is done with a needle and single thread. As we have said, the pattern is first drawn, usually upon parchment; a piece of heavy linen is stitched to the parchment for the purpose of holding it straight; then threads to the number of two, three, four, or more, are laid along the many lines of the pattern, and sewed lightly down through parchment and linen. The entire figure is then

Real Duchesse and Point Gaze.

Real Carrick=ma=Cross.

carried out, both solid filling and openwork, with fine stitching, the buttonhole stitch being most generally employed.

Bobbin, or pillow-made, lace is the highest artistic development of twisted and plaited threads. It is made from a large number of threads attached by means of pins to an oval-shaped cushion or pillow, each thread being wound upon a small bobbin. The design, as in the making of needle-point lace, is first drawn on stiff paper or parchment, and carefully stretched over the pillow. Then the pattern is pricked out along the outline of the drawing and small pins are introduced at close intervals, around which the threads work to form the various meshes and openings. From right to left the thread is bound lightly upon the bobbins and tied at the top of each in a loop that permits it gradually to slip off the bobbin when gently pulled, as occurs generally when working.

The worker begins by interlacing the bobbins, which are used in pairs, placing small pins in all perforations, and crossing the bobbins after the insertion of each pin. Around these pins the design is formed, the threads being crossed and recrossed and passed under and over each other with remarkable rapidity and accuracy. When the whole width of the large piece of lace is carried on together the number of bobbins and pins is very great and the work highly expensive, but it is customary to work each sprig separately, these being joined together in the form of a strip afterward by means of a curious loop-stitch, made by a hook called a needle-pin.

Scarcely had lace been invented before it had assumed almost priceless value, and it is worth while remarking here that though centuries have since elapsed, the value of these delicate, hand-wrought fabrics has not in any sense diminished. Throughout the sixteenth, seventeenth, eighteenth and nineteenth centuries rare lace of beautiful pattern has been highly prized, some of the earliest specimens, in the

Real Irish Point.

Real Valenciennes.

possession of world-famous libraries and museums, being of relatively fabulous wealth.

By very reason of the conditions inevitably associated with its making, lace must always remain one of the dearest articles of commerce, for there is certainly nothing more rare or costly than these fine, dainty, yet withal, substantial tissues.

Perhaps of all her compeers Venice attained the highest proficiency in the production of beautiful lace. There, as we have remarked, needle-point had its origin, and many of the beautiful patterns produced by the women of the "Queen of the Adriatic" are even to-day the admiration of all who have a true appreciation of the artistic.

Venice guarded the secret of her methods with jealous care, and it was many years before the world was made familiar with the manner in which the exquisite floral designs, with their wealth of minor adornments, were worked out. Thus Italy was able to lay tribute upon the entire civilized world, and her coffers were enriched to overflowing from the receipts of the sales of lace to eastern, central and northern Europe.

Apropos of Italy's claim to the invention of needle-point, it has been claimed that the Italians originally derived the art of fine needlework from the Greek refugees in Italy, while another author asserts that the Italians are indebted to the Saracens of Sicily for their knowledge. All these claims, however, are merely speculative. For instance, no one disputes that embroidery antedates lace, and yet we have authors who endeavor to show that embroidery had its origin in Arabia, deducing from this that lace, also, must have had its birth in one of the Oriental countries. But it is a well-established fact that while we have absolute knowledge of the existence of embroidery in the countries of the Levant, there is absolutely no indication, of even the slightest value, that points to the existence of lace before it was made by the Italians and Belgians.

In the municipal archives of Ferrara, dated 1469, is an allusion to lace, but there is a document of the Sforza family, dated in 1493, in which the word "trina" constantly occurs, together with "bone" and "bobbin" lace.

Spain was, as far as the records testify, the earliest and most adept pupil of Italy in the art of lacemaking, though, as in Italy, at the beginning the work was confined in the Iberian peninsula to the inmates of the convents. Spain, too, achieved high distinction in this field, its Point d'Espagne being one of the most celebrated of all the ancient laces, even vying with the finest Venetian point. In those days, as will be recalled, the power of the Church was absolute, and the use of laces for daily wear was prohibited, though on Sundays and holidays it was greatly in evidence in the attire of those of high station.

One of the most interesting facts concerning the development of lace has to do with the patterns produced in the various localities of Europe. In the beginning the number of designs was necessarily limited, but as the industry developed and spread, and as the workers became more expert and artistic, there was an uncontrollable impulse to break away from conventional designs and to evolve new patterns. Then, too, there was something of the spirit of pride behind this movement—a sort of local patriotism, if it may so be termed. The Belgian, the Spaniard and the Frenchman were not content slavishly to imitate Italian designs, and, anxious to win a name for themselves, set about to produce new effects that would immediately identify them with the place of their origin.

Thus it was, too, that various cities and towns in Italy, France, Belgium, Spain and elsewhere sought to establish for themselves an individual product of great excellence that would give to the city or town prestige and renown in the then few commercial marts of the world. This explains the various names which were given to distinct types of laces hundreds of years ago, and which designations still obtain, as, for instance, Alençon, Valenciennes, Chantilly, Honiton, Arras, Bayeux, Genoa, Florence, etc.

Another fact worthy of record is that of all the almost numberless designs that have been given to the world since the birth of lace there have been some one or two characteristics that tell as plainly as though expressed in words that each one of these designs was made at some particular period of history. It is well that this is so, for it has enabled the historian to trace, with more or less certainty, the development of the industry. In other words, a lace expert is enabled to tell from the fabric not only in what country it was made, but in what part of that country, and also the approximate date.

In the self-sufficiency of the present age we are apt to regard with a sort of supercilious disdain any story reflecting upon the supremacy of our forebears in any of the arts or the sciences; but that we cannot make, in a commercial way, such lace as was woven in the sixteenth and seventeenth centuries is beyond question. In the first place, time is lacking, and if it must be confessed, the great skill that comes only through years of constant practice is also lacking.

Modern real lace is artistic, even superior, but compared with such few specimens as have come down to us of the work of the lacemakers of old, its deficiency, particularly in the matter of the fineness of the execution and thread, is at once apparent. Hand-made lace is to-day produced all over the world; commercially its production is confined to France, Belgium, Germany, Spain, Italy and England, where large quantities are still produced. France, however, with that fostering care which she has bestowed upon her many other arts, and with that keen appreciation of the beautiful that is so inherent in her people, is far in the van in the matter of producing hand-made lace, though in respect to two or three types Belgium is in the front rank.

Real Honiton.

Real Florentine.

Coming down to the question of machine-made lace, it is necessary to observe at the outset that the same distinctions that exist between the genuine and the imitation do not obtain as applied to these fabrics. In other words, the knowledge that lace is a product of the frame rather than the fingers in no sense condemns it. For to such a high plane has the mechanical production of lace been lifted that one is almost tempted to say that the products vie in beauty of design and perfection of finish with the lace produced by hand. That there is warrant for this seeming exaggeration is borne out by the fact that not infrequently it is impossible for experts to tell the difference between two specimens of lace of the same design, one made by hand and the other by machine.

What inventors have accomplished in this respect is truly marvelous. In the beginning their efforts were not at all satisfactory, and the history of machine-made lace abounds with pathetic instances of men who sought in vain to duplicate with fidelity, by means of mechanical devices of hundreds of types and patterns, the dextrous touch of the human hand.

W. Felkin, in his history of lace manufacture, says that lace net was first made by machinery in 1768. Other authorities place the date as between 1758 and 1760. In 1809 bobbin net was invented, and in 1837 the Jacquard system was applied to the bobbinet machine.

Mrs. B. Palliser, in "The History of Lace," says of the invention of machinery for the production of lace that the credit is usually assigned to Hammond, a stocking framework knitter of Nottingham, who, examining one day the broad lace on his wife's cap, thought he could apply his machine to the production of a similar article. His attempt so far succeeded that, by means of the stocking frame invented in the previous century, he produced, in 1768, not lace, but a kind of knitting of running loops or stitches.

In 1777 Else and Harvey introduced at Nottingham the pin or point net machine, so named because made on sharp pins or points. Point net was followed by various other stitches of a lacelike character, but despite the progress made, all efforts at producing a solid net were futile. It was still nothing more than knitting, a single thread passing from one end of the frame to the other, and if a thread broke the work was unraveled. This was overcome in a measure by gumming the threads, giving the fabric a solidity and body not possible without resorting to some artificial method of this sort.

The great problem inspired the efforts of numberless inventors, and many attempts were made to combine the mechanism used respectively by the knitter and the weaver, and after many failures a machine was produced which made Mechlin net.

There are few histories bearing upon the invention of labor-saving devices that are so replete with the records of failure as is the history of the attempt to produce a practical lace machine. John Heathcoat, of Leicestershire, England, was the inventor of the machine for making bobbin net. His patents were taken out in 1809, and to him must be accorded the credit of solving for the first time the problem that had vexed the minds of so many inventors and had depleted the purses of so many capitalists.

The bobbin net machine, so named because the threads are wound upon bobbins, first produced a net about an inch in width, afterward, however, producing it a yard wide.

It was the application of the celebrated Jacquard attachment to the lace machine that has made possible the duplication of practically every pattern of lace made by hand. The machine of Heathcoat was vastly improved by John Leavers, also of Nottingham, and the types produced by him are still in use throughout England and France, though, of course, there are in these days a large number of different types of machines bearing different names, but the principle of the Leavers machine, more or less modified, obtains in practically all of the devices. Therefore a description of the process of lacemaking by the Leavers frame will serve as a description for all.

The number of threads brought into operation in this machine is regulated by the pattern to be produced. The threads are of two sorts, warp and bobbin threads. Upward of 9,000 are sometimes used, sixty pieces of lace being made at once, each piece requiring 148 threads (100 warps and 48 bobbin threads). The supply of warp threads is held upon reels, the bobbins carrying their own supply. The warp threads are stretched perpendicularly and about wide enough apart to admit a silver quarter passing edgeways between them. The bobbins are flattened in shape so as to pass conveniently between the warps. Each bobbin can contain about 120 yards of thread. By most ingenious mechanism varying degrees of tension can be imparted to warp and bobbin threads as required. The bobbins, as they pass like pendulums between the warp threads, are made to oscillate, and through this oscillation the threads twist themselves or become twisted with the warp threads, as required by the pattern that is being produced. As the twisting takes place, combs compress the twistings, making them more compact. If the bobbin threads be made tight and the warp threads slack, the latter will be twisted upon the former; but if the warps are brought to a tension and the bobbin threads be slack, then the latter will be twisted on the warps. The combs are so regulated that they come clear away from the threads as soon as they have pressed them together, and fall into position ready to perform their pressing operations again. The contrivances for giving each thread a particular tension and movement at a certain time are connected with an adaptation of the Jacquard system of pierced cards. The lace machine is highly complicated, much of its complexity being due to the mechanism

Real Point Appliqué.

by which the oscillating or lateral movements are produced. Expert workmen prepare the working drawings for the lace machine, and also perform the more important duties in its operation, but a large part of the work is carried on by women and girls.

One of the most interesting developments of the lace industry has been the gradual evolution from the work of the hand toilers to the utilization of complex machinery. In addition to the Leavers machine, which is referred to elsewhere in extenso, the embroidery machine plays a very important part in the making of laces. From 1870 to 1880, various efforts had been made to produce lace on the embroidery machine, and it was during this decade that the first success was achieved in the making of Oriental or net laces in Plauen. This was the first actual production of lace from the embroidering machine, and this sort of lace, which still exists to-day, is really an embroidery on a net, although usually designated as lace. A few years later a discovery was made which effected a great change in the making of laces on the embroidery machine. This was the principle of embroidering on a material which was afterward removed by a chemical process. The first article produced was called Guipure de Genes, and was at that time patented, but the patent was held to be invalid, and a few years afterward this article was generally produced both in St. Gall, where it first appeared, and in Plauen. By this method of manufacture are produced to-day all of the imitation guipure laces, such as Point de Venise, Rose Point, Point de Genes, etc.

The embroidering machine in use at the present day is constructed entirely of iron, measuring from 15 to 20 feet long, 9 feet high, 9 feet wide and weighs about 3,800 pounds. It can be operated by hand or by power. The method of embroidering is exceedingly simple. The cloth, usually somewhat over $4\frac{1}{2}$ yards long, is tightly stretched in an upright position in the center of the machine, each end of the suspended

Real Chantilly.

Real Spanish.

strip being held firmly by means of stout hooks. The needles (from 150 to 300 in number, according to the sort of work to be done) are arranged horizontally in a framework in a straight, level row, all pointing toward the cloth and extending from end to end of same. The needles are supplied with threads about one yard in length, which are fastened by means of a peculiar knot to the eye, the latter being in the middle of the needle instead of at the end. In producing any given stitch in the pattern to be worked, the long row of needles all move forward at once at the will of the operator, and thus duplicate the stitch in every pattern or "section" along the entire $4\frac{1}{2}$ yards of cloth suspended in the machine. As may be readily understood, the machine in this manner completes $4\frac{1}{2}$ yards of embroidery in the same time it would take a woman with a needle to finish a single pattern. When one row is completed the strip of cloth is raised and another row is made, and so on until it is necessary to put in another length of cambric. This machine is capable of making patterns from the very narrow up to the full width of the cloth.

What is known as the Schiffli, or power machine, is very similar to the hand-embroidering device, being an improvement on the latter and worked with a shuttle in addition to the needles. Its capacity is nearly eight times greater, or from 15,000 to 18,000 stitches per day, against 2,000 to 3,000 on the hand machine. To offset this advantage, however, the Schiffli machine is much more expensive, and is of delicate and complicated construction, easily got out of order and costly to repair. Until a comparatively recent date the Schiffli was not considered as a competitor of the hand machine, its work being inferior in quality and confined to simple patterns. At present, however, it is generally conceded that the goods produced by it not only compete with the hand-machine products, but are already superseding the latter to some extent. It is predicted that the Schiffli machine, operated by power, will ultimately supply all the embroidery in the low and medium grades.

The variety and adaptability of the designs which both of these machines are capable of producing are endless, and at the same time comparatively inexpensive. It is this latter fact which accounts for the great advantage of the embroidering machine over the lace machine. The preparing and setting of a design for a lace machine is very expensive, and the great cost compels the manufacturer of machine lace to turn out large quantities of one set pattern in order to get a return from his investment.

About the beginning of the nineteenth century, lace machines were first introduced into France from Nottingham, at Boulogne-sur-mer, where the industry remained for a few years and then moved to Calais. There this industry has developed and increased to such proportions that Calais is now the principal city for the production of fine laces of all kinds, and practically leads Nottingham in creating novelties and new and original effects. Shortly after the Franco-Prussian war the industry found a foothold in Caudry, in the north of France, where it has also developed to quite large proportions, and shares to-day a large part of the trade which has resulted from the founding of the parent industry in Calais. The kind of lace produced in Caudry is generally of a cheaper character than that produced in Calais.

In Lyons, too, there has been established for many years the industry of making laces and nettings by mechanical processes. This is still a very large industry, and about twenty years ago there was a large trade done with America in the manufacture of laces in vogue at that time, which were the imitation of the real Spanish, called "Blonde Grenade." There are still made in Lyons to-day various imitations of fine laces, which in a general way are of a different quality to the laces made at Calais or Caudry, and Lyons enjoys a reputation in regard to the character of the laces it produces which is unique in the trade.

About the year 1890, a Frenchman invented a machine similar in principle to the knitting machine, which reproduces with absolute fidelity the work of the bobbins in making pillow laces. Through this invention he was able to imitate such hand-made laces as Torchons, Medicis, etc., so exactly that experts could not detect the difference. In fact, it is the general testimony of men associated with laces for years, that the work of this machine in a great many of its aspects is one of the most important contributions of the mechanical arts in the production of lace.

Through the importation of foreign machines and foreign workmen, various attempts have been made in the United States to establish the manufacture of lace. At the present writing it is impossible to state with any definiteness what the result will be, as the experiment has been of only a few years' duration, and in the very nature of things is at this date of a tentative character.

In order that the reader may be able to distinguish the various types of hand and machine made laces, we append herewith a glossary, defining as concisely as possible the characteristics that indicate not only the manifold makes of laces, but what may be called the various sub-divisions. These definitions are set forth, the writer hopes, in terms that will enable the reader to understand what each one of the various names means, both as applied commercially and descriptively.

Real Point Gaze.

Imitation Duchesse.

CHARACTERISTICS OF THE DIFFERENT TYPES OF LACE.

ALENÇON.—A fine, needle-point lace, so called from Alençon, a French city, in which its manufacture was first begun. It is the only French lace not made upon the pillow, the work being done entirely by hand, with a fine needle, upon a parchment pattern in small pieces. The pieces are afterward united by invisible seams. There are usually twelve processes, including the design employed in the production of a piece of this kind of lace, and each of these processes is executed by a special workwoman; but in 1855, at Bayeux, in France, a departure was made from the old custom of assigning a special branch of the work to each lacemaker, and the fabric was made through all its processes by one worker.

The design is engraved upon a copper plate and then printed off upon pieces of green parchment of a specified length. After the pattern is pricked upon the parchment, which is stitched to a piece of coarse linen folded double, the pattern is then formed in outline by guiding two flat threads along the edge by the thumb of the left hand, and, in order to fix it, minute stitches are made with another thread and needle through the holes of the parchment. After the outline is finished it is given to another worker to make the ground, which is chiefly of two kinds: bride, consisting of uniting threads which serve to join together the flowers of the lace, and réseau, which is worked backward and forward from the footing to the picot. There was also another ground called Argentella, consisting of buttonhole-stitched skeleton hexagons.

In making the flowers of Alençon point, the workwoman, using a needle and fine thread, makes the buttonhole-stitch from left to right, and, when she has reached the end of the flower, throws back the thread from the point of departure and works again from left to right along the thread. As a result, the work is characterized by a closeness, firmness and evenness not equaled in any other point lace.

When the work is completed the threads which bind lace, linen and parchment together are carefully cut, and the difficult task of uniting the pieces together remains to be done. This is accomplished by means of what is called the "assemblage" stitch, instead of the "point de raccroc," where the pieces are united by a fresh row of stitches.

Another way of uniting the pieces, which is used at Alençon, is by a seam which follows as far as possible the outlines of the pattern so as to be invisible. A steel instrument, called a picot, is then passed into each flower so as to give it a more finished appearance.

Alençon point is of a durability which no other lace can rival. A peculiarity in its manufacture is, that it is the only lace in which horsehair is inserted along the edge to give increased strength to the cordonnet, a practice originating in the necessity of making the point stand up when the tall headdresses formerly worn by women were exposed to the wind.

Formerly Alençon point, notwithstanding its beauty of construction, could not vie with Brussels lace as regards the excellence of floral design, but this inferiority has now been removed by the production of exquisite copies of natural flowers, mingled with grasses and ferns. Alençon point is now made not only at the seat of its original manufacture, but at Bayeux, at Burano, near Venice, and at Brussels.

Bayeux can boast of one of the finest examples of this lace ever made. It was exhibited in 1867, and consisted of a dress of two flounces, in which the pattern, flowers and foliage were most harmoniously wrought and relieved by shaded tints, which give to the lace the relief of a picture. The price of the dress was $17,000, and it took forty women seven years to finish it.

The city of Alençon had on exhibition at Paris, in 1899, a piece of lace of exquisite description, that had taken 16,500 working days to complete.

ALLOVER.—Lace of any kind which is eighteen inches or more in width, and used for yokes, flouncings and entire costumes.

ANTIQUE.—A pillow lace, hand-made from heavy linen thread, and characterized by an exceedingly open, coarse, square mesh. It is mainly used for curtains, bed sets and draperies.

ANTWERP.—A pillow lace made at Antwerp, resembling early Alençon, and whose chief characteristic is the representation of a pot or vase of flowers with which it is always decorated. The pot or vase varies much in size and details. It is usually grounded with a coarse "Fond Champ."

APPLICATION.—A lace made by sewing flowers or sprigs, which may be either needle-point or bobbin-made, upon a bobbin-lace ground. One variety of Brussels lace affords the best example of Application.

APPLIQUÉ.—The same as Application lace.

ARGENTAN.—A needle-point lace, usually considered indistinguishable from Alençon, but which is different in some respects, its marked peculiarity being that the réseau ground is not made of single threads only, but the sides of each mesh are worked over with the buttonhole stitch. Argentan is often distinguished from Alençon lace by a larger and more striking pattern, and in some instances it is especially known by its hexagonally arranged brides. It is called after Argentan, a town near Alençon, and the lace was made there under the same direction.

ARRAS.—A white pillow lace, so called from Arras, in France, the city of its original manufacture. It is simple and almost uniform in design, very strong and firm to the touch, and comparatively cheap in price. It is made on a lisle ground. The older and finer patterns of Arras lace reached their climax of excellence during the first Empire, between 1804 and 1812, but since then they have gone out of fashion.

Real Duchesse.

Real Irish Crochet.

AURILLAC.—A pillow or bobbin lace, made at Aurillac, in France. In the early period of its manufacture it was a close-woven fabric, resembling the guipure of Genoa and Flanders, but later it resembled English point. The laces of Aurillac ended with the Revolution.

AUVERGNE.—A pillow lace made at the French city of Auvergne and the surrounding district.

AVE MARIA.—A narrow lace used for edging. (See Dieppe lace.)

BABY.—A narrow lace used for edging, and made principally in the English counties of Bedfordshire, Buckinghamshire and Northamptonshire. These laces are ordinarily of simple design and specially employed in adorning infants' caps. Though this fashion went out in Great Britain, the ladies of America held to the trimmed infants' caps until the breaking out of the Civil War, and up to that date large quantities of this lace were exported to America.

BASKET.—A lace so woven or plaited as to resemble basket-work. It is mentioned in inventories of 1580.

BAYEUX.—There are two descriptions of lace known by this name: (a) A modern pillow lace, made at Bayeux, in Normandy, particularly the variety made in imitation of Rose point; (b) A black silk lace, popular because made in unusually large pieces, as for shawls, fichus, etc.

BISETTE.—A narrow, coarse-thread pillow lace of three qualities, formerly made in the suburbs of Paris by the peasant women, principally for their own use. The name is now used to signify narrow bordering lace of small value.

BOBBIN.—Lace made on a pillow, stuffed so as to form a cushion, without the use of a needle. A stiff piece of parchment is fixed on the pillow, and after holes are pricked through the parchment so as to form the pattern small pins are stuck through these holes into the pillow. The threads with which the lace is formed are wound upon bobbins—small, round pieces of wood about the size of a pencil, having round

Real Irish Appliqué.

Imitation Point de Venise.

their upper ends a deep groove, so formed as to reduce the bobbin to a thin neck, on which the thread is wound, a separate bobbin being used for each thread. The ground of the lace is formed by the twisting and crossing of these threads. The pattern or figure, technically called "gimp," is made by interweaving a thread much thicker than that forming the groundwork, according to the design pricked out on the parchment. This manner of using the pillow in lacemaking has remained practically the same during more than three centuries.

BLONDE.—A lace so-called because, being made from raw silk, it was "fair," not white in color. Blonde lace has a "réseau" of the Lille type, made of fine twisted silk, the "toile" being worked entirely with a broad, flat strand, producing a very attractive glistening effect. It was made at Chantilly, in France. At the Revolution the demand for this fabric ceased, as lacemakers were commonly looked upon as royal protégés. During the First Empire, however, blonde became fashionable again, and since that time the popularity of black silk blonde for Spanish mantillas alone has kept the trade in a flourishing condition. The manufacture is not confined to any one town, but is carried on throughout the province of Calvados, in Normandy, and is also made in Spain.

BOBBINET.—A variety of Application lace, in which the pattern is applied upon a ground of bobbinet or tulle.

BONE POINT.—A lace without a regular mesh ground.

BORDER.—Lace made in long, narrow pieces, with a footing on one side, the other edge being ordinarily Van Dyked or purled. During the larger part of the seventeenth century a constant supply of this lace was made at Genoa. It was commonly called "Collar" lace, from the use to which it was put. In the pictures of Rubens and Van Dyke it is frequently represented as trimming the broad falling linen collars, both of men and elderly women. It can be distinguished from Flemish lace, also employed in the same way, by its greater boldness of design.

Younger women also made use of it as trimming for the shoulders of their décolleté dresses, and also for sleeves, aprons, etc.

BRIDE.—Lace whose ground is wholly composed of brides or bars, without a réseau or net.

BRUSSELS.—A celebrated lace, made at and near Brussels, in Belgium; more particularly, a fine variety of the lace made there whose pattern, as compared with Alençon, has less relief, and whose fine net ground is without "picots," the knots or thorns which often decorate "brides," and also the edge of the pattern. Brussels lace, whose history is one of the most interesting in the progress of this industry, is now often regarded as an application lace, by reason of the fact that the laceworkers of that city, after machine-made net had been perfected by an English invention in 1810, adopted the plan of appliquéing their pillow-made patterns on that material. Lace so appliquéd can be recognized as distinct from that made with the "vrai réseau," or true network ground, by the fact that the net ground, though sometimes removed, is often seen to pass behind the lace pattern, and also by the character of the network. Machine-made net is composed of diamond-shaped meshes, and is made with two threads only, tightly twisted and crossed, not plaited, at their junction, and is quite unlike the Brussels pillow "réseau." Other peculiarities by which Brussels lace may be recognized are: (a) It is not made in one piece on the pillow, but the pattern is first made by itself, and the "réseau" ground is worked in around it afterward. (b) The "réseau" ground, when magnified under a glass, has a mesh of hexagonal form, of which two sides are made of four threads plaited four times, and four sides of two threads twisted twice. (c) Brussels pillow lace has two sorts of "toilé," or substance of the pattern as contrasted with the groundwork; one, the usual woven texture, resembling that of a piece of cambric; the other, a more open arrangement of open threads, having very much the appearance of the Fond Champ "réseau." It remains to be said, in spite of the fact that the above-mentioned characteristics may always be distinguished, that the Brussels pillow lace of the present day differs materially from the earlier forms, having gone through many changes and style in pattern and make. Among these are Point d'Angleterre, called such for mistaken reasons only, as it is not point lace nor made in England; and Duchesse, a name of comparatively recent date, though the style itself is of earlier origin, and was called "Guipure façon Angleterre." As regards Brussels needle-point, the earliest made closely resembles that of Alençon, though not quite so close and firm. There were also other differences, both the "cordonnet" and the "réseau" being unlike those of Alençon. From the beginning of the nineteenth century Brussels needle-point underwent changes analogous to those of pillow lace; it became Point Appliqué, in which the needle-lace pattern, instead of having a true net ground, was appliquéd on the machine-made net. But in recent years it has been noted that a return to the character of the earlier and more beautiful Brussels needle-point is being sought, the chief evidence of it being the exquisite Point Gaze, made entirely with the needle and grounded with its own "réseau."

BUCKINGHAM.—A lace originally made in the county of Buckingham, England, and of two kinds: (a) Buckingham trolley lace, whose pattern is outlined with a thicker thread, or a flat, narrow border, made up of several such threads. The ground is usually a double ground, showing hexagonal and triangular meshes; (b) A lace with a point ground, with the pattern outlined with thicker threads, these threads being weighted by bobbins larger and heavier than the rest. In general character and design these laces strongly resemble those manufactured at Lille.

CADIZ.—A variety of needle-point Brussels lace.

Imitation Marquise.

Real Point d'Angleterre.

CARNIVAL.—A variety of reticella lace made in Italy, Spain and France during the sixteenth century.

CARTISANE.—Guipure or passement, made with cartisane, which is vellum or parchment in thin strips or small rolls, covered with silk, gold thread or similar material.

CHAIN.—A lace of the seventeenth century, consisting of a braid or passement so worked as to resemble chain links. It was made of colored silk, and also of gold and silver thread.

CHANTILLY.—One of the blonde laces, of the sort recognizable by their Alençon réseau ground and the flowers in light or openwork instead of solid. It is made both in white and black silk. Black Chantilly lace has always been made of silk, but a grenadine, not a lustrous silk. The pattern is outlined with a cordonnet of a flat, untwisted silk strand. During the seventeenth century the Duchesse of Longueville established the manufacture of silk lace at Chantilly and its neighborhood, and as Paris was near and the demand of royalty for this lace increased it became very popular. At the time of the Revolution the prosperity of the industry was ruined, and many of the lacemakers were sent to the guillotine. During the ascendancy of the first Napoleon, the manufacture of Chantilly again became flourishing. Since then the industry has been driven away from that town on account of the higher labor costs resulting from the nearness of Chantilly to Paris, and the lacemakers, unable to meet this increased cost, retired to Gisors, where half a century ago there were between 8,000 and 10,000 lacemakers. The supremacy of lacemaking formerly enjoyed by Chantilly has now been trasferred to Calvados, Caen, Bayeux and Grammont. The widely-known Chantilly shawls are made at Bayeux, and also at Grammont.

CHENILLE.—A French lace, made in the eighteenth century, so called because the patterns were outlined with fine white chenille. The ground was made of silk in honeycomb réseau, and the patterns were geometrical and filled with thick stitches.

CLUNY.—A kind of net lace with a square net background in which the stitch is darned. It is so called from the famous museum of antiquities in the Hôtel Cluny, at Paris, and also because the lace was supposed to have a medieval appearance. The patterns used are generally of an antique and quaint description, mostly of birds, animals and flowers, and in the existing manufacture the old traditions are fairly well preserved. Sometimes a glazed thread is introduced in the pattern as an outline. Cluny is a plaited lace, somewhat similar to the Genoese and Maltese laces, and is made in silk, linen or cotton.

CORDOVER.—A kind of filling used in the pattern of ancient and modern point lace.

CORK.—A name formerly used for Irish lace in general, when the manufacture of Irish lace was principally confined to the neighborhood of Cork.

CRAPONNE.—A kind of stout thread guipure lace, of cheap price and inferior make, used for furniture.

CRETAN.—A name given to an old lace, ordinarily made of colored material, whether silk or linen, and sometimes embroidered with the needle after the lace was complete.

CREWEL.—A kind of edging made of crewel or worsted thread, intended as a border or binding for garments.

CROCHET.—Lace which is made with a crochet hook, or whose pattern is so made and then appliquéd on a bobbin or machine-made net. It is similar to needle-point lace, although not equal in fineness to the best examples of the latter.

CROWN.—A lace whose pattern was worked on a succession of crowns, sometimes intermixed with acorns and roses. It was made first in the reign of Queen Elizabeth. A relic of this lace may still be found in the "faux galon," sold for the decoration of fancy dresses and theatrical purposes.

DALECARLIAN.—Lace made for their own use by the peasants of Dalecarlia, a province of Sweden. Its patterns are ancient and traditional. It is a coarse guipure lace, made of unbleached thread.

DAMASCENE.—An imitation of Honiton lace, made by joining lace sprigs and lace braid with corded bars. It differs from modern point lace in that it has real Honiton sprigs, and is without needlework fillings.

DARNED LACE.—A general name for lace upon a net ground, upon which the pattern is appliquéd in needlework. The different laces of this kind are described under Filet Brodé, Guipure d'Art and Spiderwork.

DEVONSHIRE.—Lace made in Devonshire, England, and more frequently designated as Honiton. (See Honiton.) Formerly practically the whole female population of Devonshire were employed in lacemaking, and during the sixteenth and seventeenth centuries Belgian, French and Spanish laces were imitated in that country most successfully, as were also Venetian and Spanish needle-point, Maltese, Greek and Genoese laces. During the last century this variety in lacemaking has died out in Devonshire, and now only Honiton is made.

DIAMOND.—A lace made with a stitch either worked as open or close diamonds, and used in modern point and in ancient needle-points.

DIEPPE.—A fine point lace made at Dieppe, in France, resembling Valenciennes, and made with three threads instead of four. There were several kinds of lace made at Dieppe in the seventeenth and eighteenth centuries, including Brussels, Mechlin, Point de Paris and Valenciennes, but the true Dieppe point was eventually restricted to two kinds, the narrow being called the Ave Maria and Poussin, the wider and double grounded, the Dentelle à la Vierge. Dieppe and

Real Torchon.

Imitation Valenciennes.

Havre were formerly the two great lace centers of Normandy, manufacturing in those cities having antedated that at Alençon, but the prosperity of the lace industry in both these cities was nearly destroyed at the Revolution, and though for a time encouraged under the restored Bourbons, and patronized by Napoleon III, machine-made laces have practically driven the old Dieppe point out of the market.

DRESDEN POINT.—A fine drawn lace, embroidered with the needle and made in Dresden during the latter part of the seventeenth and the whole of the eighteenth century. It was an imitation of an Italian point lace, in which a piece of linen was converted into lace by some of its threads being drawn away, some retained to form a pattern, and others worked together to form square meshes. The manufacture of Dresden point declined, and now laces of many kinds are made there, notably an imitation of old Brussels.

DUCHESSE.—A fine pillow lace, a variety originally made in Belgium resembling Honiton guipure lace in design and workmanship, but worked with a finer thread and containing a greater amount of raised or relief work. The leaves, flowers and sprays formed are larger and of bolder design. The stitches and manner of working in Honiton and Duchesse are alike.

DUNKIRK.—A pillow lace made with a flat thread, and whose manufacture was carried on in the districts around Dunkirk, a French seaport, in the seventeenth century. The best known kind was an imitation of Mechlin lace.

DUTCH.—A coarse, strong lace, made with a thick ground, and of plain and heavy design. It is a kind of cheap Valenciennes. Dutch lace is inferior in design and workmanship to those of France and Belgium.

ENGLISH POINT.—(a) A fine pillow lace made in the eighteenth century, generally considered to be of Flemish origin and manufacture, and mistakenly called "Point d'Angleterre," as it was neither point lace nor made in England. Some writers, however, assert its English origin. Owing to the protection formerly given by law to English laces, large quantities of Belgium laces are believed to have been smuggled into England under the name of "Point d'Angleterre," so as to evade the customs duties. (b) At the present day the finest quality of Brussels lace, in which needle-point sprigs are applied to Brussels bobbin-ground. (See Application lace, also Point d'Angleterre.)

ESCURIAL.—A modern silk lace, made in imitation of Rose point. The patterns are outlined with a lustrous thread or cord.

FAYAL.—A delicately made and costly lace, hand-made by the women of the Island of Fayal, one of the Azores, off the western Spanish coast. The thread used in making this lace is spun from the fiber of the leaves of the alol, a plant resembling somewhat the century plant. Great skill is necessary in the manufacture, which is restricted to a comparatively few women of the island, who have been trained to this work from childhood. The lace is marketed in France, chiefly in Paris, at a very high price, and it is very difficult for outside purchasers to buy it at any cost. The patterns are extremely elegant and original in design. Notwithstanding the delicacy of this fabric, it is remarkably durable.

FEDORA.—See Point Appliqué.

FALSE VALENCIENNES.—(a) Lace resembling Valenciennes in surface and in pattern, but without the true Valenciennes net ground. (b) A term for Valenciennes lace made in Belgium.

FLAT POINT.—Lace made without any raised-work or work in relief from raised points.

FLEMISH POINT.—A needle-point guipure lace made in Flanders.

FOOTING.—A narrow lace which is used to keep the stitches of the ground firm and to sew the lace to the garment upon which it is to be worn. Sometimes the footing is worked with the rest of the design. It is used also in making lace handkerchiefs and for quilling effects.

Genoa.—A name originally given to the gold and silver laces for which Genoa was famed in the sixteenth and seventeenth centuries, but now applied to lace made from the fiber of the aloe plant, and also to Macramé lace.

Gold.—Lace made of warp threads or cords of silk, or silk and cotton combined, with thin gold or silver gilt bands passing around it. It was anciently made of gold or silver gilt wire. It is now used chiefly to decorate uniforms, liveries and some church costumes, and occasionally for millinery. The metal is drawn through a wire, and, after being flattened between steel rollers, several strands of the flattened wire are passed around the silk simultaneously by means of a complex machine having a wheel and iron bobbins. The history of gold lace is interesting, as illustrating the oldest form of the lacemaker's art. From the days of Egypt and Rome down to medieval Venice, Italy and Spain, gold and silver gilt wire were used in making this kind of lace. The Jews in Spain were accomplished workers in this art, and in Sweden and Russia gold lace was the first lace made. In France gold lacemaking was a prosperous manufacture at Aurrillac and Arras, at which latter place it flourished up to the end of the eighteenth century. Gold lace was imported into England at an early date, and King James I established a monopoly in it. Its importation was prohibited by Queen Anne, on account of the extravagant uses of ornamentation to which it was put, and it was also prohibited in the reign of George II, to correct the prevalent taste for the foreign manufactured lace. The attempt was unsuccessful, for we are told that smuggling greatly increased. It became a "war to the knife between the revenue officer and society at large, all classes combined, town ladies of high degree, with waiting-

Real Mechlin.

Real Point de Paris.

maids, and the common sailor, to avoid the obnoxious duties and cheat the government."

GRAMMONT.—Grammont lace, so called from the town of Grammont, in Belgium, where it was originally manufactured, is of two kinds: (a) A cheap, white pillow lace. (b) A black silk lace, resembling the Chantilly blondes. These laces are made for flounces and shawls, and were used both in America and Europe. As compared with Chantilly, the ground is coarser and the patterns are not so clear-cut and elegant as the real Chantilly.

GUEUSE.—A thread pillow lace made in France during the eighteenth century. The ground of this lace was réseau, and the toilé was worked with a thicker thread than the ground. It was formerly an article of extensive consumption in France, but, after the beginning of the nineteenth century, it was little used, except by the poorer classes. It was formerly called "Beggars' lace."

GUIPURE.—It was originally a kind of lace or passement made of cartisane and twisted silk. The name was afterward applied to heavy lace made with thin wires whipped around the silk, and with cotton thread. The word guipure is no longer commonly used to denote such work as this, but has become a term of variable designation, and it is so extensively applied that it is difficult to give a limit to its meaning. It may be used to define a lace where the flowers are either joined by brides, or large coarse stitches, or lace that has no ground. The modern Honiton and Maltese are guipures, and so is Venetian point. But as the word has also been applied to large, flowing pattern laces, worked with coarse net grounds, it is impossible to lay down any hard and fast rule about it.

HENRIQUES.—A fine stitch or point, used both in early and modern needle-point work.

HOLLIE POINT.—A needle-point lace said to have been originally

Real Arabian.

Machine Irish Crochet.

called holy point, on account of its uses. It was popular in the middle ages for church decoration, but was adapted to different purposes in the seventeenth and eighteenth centuries, and various makes of lace have since been called by this name.

HONITON.—A pillow lace originally made at Honiton, Devonshire, England, and celebrated for the beauty of its figures and sprigs. The manufacture is still carried on at that town, where there is a lace school, but a similar lace is made in the leading Continental centers of the industry.

(a) Honiton Application is made by working the pattern parts on the lace pillow and securing them to a net ground, separately made. At present it is customary to use machine-made net upon which hand-made sprays are sewn.

(b) Honiton guipure, which in common acceptation passes as Honiton lace, is distinguished by its large flower patterns upon a very open ground, the sprays being united by brides or bars.

Honiton braid is a narrow, machine-made fabric, the variety in most general use being composed of a series of oval-shaped figures united by narrow bars. It is of different widths, in linen, cotton and silk, and is much used in the manufacture of handkerchiefs, collars, and some varieties of lace.

The history of Honiton lace is more than ordinarily interesting, partly by reason of the doubt as to whether it really was a lace of English invention, or brought by the Flemish workmen to England. Some writers assert the former, but the stronger probability is that the art was brought from Flanders by Protestant immigrants, who fled from persecution. Whichever theory is held, the development of the industry at Honiton, and its close resemblance to other lacemaking processes in Belgium, Holland and France, afford an excellent illustration of the interdependence of lacemakers in all countries upon each other as regards improvements resulting from new ideas. Honiton, if it was brought from Flanders originally, afterward repaid the debt by the beauty and celebrity of its designs, which served as examples for Continental lacemakers. The very attempt to protect its manufacture in England, by imposing prohibitive duties, only increased the desire to receive foreign suggestions, and to smuggle foreign laces into England, while the ingenuity of Continental manufacturers succeeded in copying the best Honiton designs, and even in improving upon them. The English lacemakers at Honiton were, however, at first unsuccessful in their attempts to rival the best laces of the Continent, especially Brussels. Although they had royal patronage, and the whims and lavish expenditure of the court of Charles II were at their service, together with protective duties, it was not until the reign of George II and George III that English lace substantially improved. This resulted from substituting the working of the true Brussels net ground, or vrai réseau, for the old guipure bar ground. The patterns were also formed of detached flower sprays, and soon the Honiton product became almost unrivaled. This superiority continued until about 1820, when machine-made net was introduced, and the old exquisite net ground, made of the finest Antwerp thread, went out of fashion by reason of the commercial demand for an inferior product. Honiton guipure is now the chief form of lace made at that town. As regards composition of the patterns of Honiton laces, as well as finish and delicacy of execution, much improvement has been manifested during the last twenty years by reason of better schools for design, and the rivalry promoted by international exhibitions.

IMITATION.—Machine-made lace of any kind. It often rivals real lace in fineness, but necessarily its mechanical regularity of pattern detracts somewhat from the artistic character of the result. Constant improvement in processes, however, has in some laces made the resemblance to the hand-made product so close that even experts can hardly recognize the difference. If it were asked how the imitation lace can be distinguished from needle-point, the answer is that it is not made with looped stitches like the latter, nor has it the effect of plaited threads, as in pillow lace. Again, the toilé of machine-made lace is often found to be ribbed, and this lace is very generally made of cotton instead of the linen thread with which old needle-point and pillow lace is made. In the invention of substitutes for hand-made lace stitches Switzerland has been the leader, and by 1868 hundreds of machines, perfected from the invention of a native of St. Gall, were turning out a close imitation of the hand-made work. The most recent triumphs of this description are the imitations of Venetian point, in which a nearer approximation than ever before has been made to the needle-worked toilé, and also of the bride work. But, notwithstanding the marvelous results attained in machine-made lace, they are the triumphs of mechanism which cannot displace the superiority, and charm, and rarity, of the finest hand-made work. In the latter the personal equation, the skill and the loving, workmanlike fidelity of the individual toiler to his task impart a quality which dead mechanism can neither create nor supersede. Machine-made lace may be predominantly the lace of commerce, but hand-made lace is the natural expression and embodiment of a delicate and difficult art, and thus it will ever remain.

INSERTION.—A kind of lace, embroidery or other trimming used to insert in a plain fabric for ornamental purposes. It is made with the edges on both sides alike, and often a plain portion of the material outside the work, so that it may be sewn on one side to the garment for which it is intended and to the plain part of the lace or border on the other.

IRISH.—A term denoting a variety of laces made in Ireland, of which the two most individual and best-known kinds are the net em-

Imitation Point d'Alençon.

broideries of Limerick and the appliqué and cut cambric work of Carrick-ma-cross. Other varieties, which are imitations of foreign laces, are Irish point, resembling Brussels lace; black and white Maltese; silver, black and white blondes. The Limerick embroideries, for they cannot be strictly called lace, are an imitation of Indian tambour work, and consist of fine embroidery in chain-stitches upon a Nottingham net. Carrick-ma-cross, or Irish guipure, is a kind of so-called Irish point lace, made at the town of that name, but which is really nothing more than a species of embroidery, from which part of the cloth is cut away, leaving a guipure ground. It is not a very durable lace. The most popular patterns are the rose and the shamrock. Irish crochet is an imitation of the needle-point laces of Spain and Venice; that is to say, it resembles these laces in general effect. There is also a needle-point lace made of rather coarse thread, and used exclusively in Ireland and England. The manufacture of laces in Ireland is carried on by the cottagers, by the nuns in the convents, and in several industrial schools founded for that purpose. It has only become a popular industry within the last twenty-five years, as the costumes of the people in earlier times did not require lace ornamentation, and there was a widespread and deep-rooted aversion to the adoption of English fashions in clothing so long as certain sumptuary laws were unrepealed.

Afterward, under slightly more liberal conditions, English fashions were gradually adopted, and with them came the demand for a cheap Irish lace, as the foreign laces were too expensive. Not until 1743 was there any official attempt to encourage the industry, but in that year the Royal Dublin Society established prizes for excellence in lacemaking. This attempt lasted until 1774. In 1829 a school was opened in Limerick for instruction in the now celebrated lace or embroidery first made in that town; but in the famine years of 1846-48 more effectual measures were taken to spread a knowledge of the art, and several schools were opened in different parts of the country. The Irish have never made a lace that can in any sense be called national, but great skill has been developed in the imitations of the foreign fabrics, and the Irish name has been so closely associated with some of them that they are popularly considered a native Irish product. The exhibition of Irish laces at the Mansion House in London in 1883 added materially to the reputation of these fabrics.

IRISH TRIMMING.—A plain-patterned, woven lace, formerly used in ornamenting muslin underwear, pillow slips and the like.

JESUIT.—A modern needle-point lace, made in Ireland, and so called on account of the tradition as to the introduction of its manufacture after the famine of 1846.

KNOTTED.—A term applied to the old Punto a Groppo, of Italian manufacture originally, and consisting of a fringe or border made of knotted threads. It is commonly called Knotting in all English-speaking countries. The modern Macramé is made like the knotted laces.

LILLE.—A lace made at Lille, in France, noted for its clear and light single réseau ground, which is sometimes ornamented with points d'esprit. It is a lace of simple design, consisting of a thick run thread, enclosing cloth-stitch for thick parts, and plaitings for open parts. The old Lille lace is always made with a stiff and formal pattern, with a thick, straight edge, and with a square instead of the usual round dots worked over the ground. Lille was distinguished as a lacemaking city as far back as 1582, and from that year until 1848 the industry was successful, but since the latter year there has been a steady decline, as more remunerative occupations have gradually drawn away the younger workers from lacemaking. The Lille pattern was similar to that of the laces made at Arras and Mirecourt, in France, and in Bedfordshire and Buckinghamshire, in England, but none of the latter could rival the famous single réseau ground.

LIMERICK.—(See Irish Lace.)

LUXEUIL.—A term applied to several varieties of hand-made lace produced at Luxeuil, France. They are stout, heavy laces, mostly made with the use of braid, and are much used for curtains and draperies.

MACRAMÉ.—A word of Arabic derivation, signifying a fringe for trimming, whether cotton, thread or silk, and now used to designate an ornamental cotton trimming, sometimes called a lace, made by leaving a long fringe of coarse thread, and interweaving the threads so as to make patterns geometrical in form. It is useful in decorating light upholstery. Macramé cord is made of fine, close-twisted cotton thread, prepared especially for the manufacture of Macramé trimming, and also for coarse netting of various kinds. The foundation of all Macramé lace or trimming is knots, made by tying short ends of thread either in horizontal or perpendicular lines, and interweaving the knots so as to form a geometrical design, as above mentioned, and sometimes raised, sometimes flat. This necessitates the forming of simple patterns. This lace is really a revival of the old Italian knotted points, which were much used three centuries ago in Spain and Italy for ecclesiastical garments. It appears in some of the paintings of the early masters, notably Paul Veronese. The art has been taught during all the nineteenth century in the schools and convents along the Riviera. It is developed in great perfection at Chiavari, and also at Genoa. Specimens of elaborate workmanship were in the Paris Exhibition of 1867.

MACKLIN.—Another name for Mechlin lace.

MALINE.—A name sometimes applied to Mechlin lace, especially to the varieties whose ground is distinguished by a diamond-shaped mesh.

MALTESE.—A heavy but attractive pillow lace, whose patterns, of arabesque or geometric design, are formed of plaiting or cloth-stitch, and are united with a purled bar ground. It is made both in white silk

Real Cluny.

Real Bruges.

and thread, and also in black Barcelona silk. There is also a cotton machine-made variety, used chiefly in trimming muslin underwear. The history of Maltese lace is interesting from the fact that the kind originally made in that island by the natives, which was a coarse variety of Mechlin or Valenciennes, of an arabesque pattern, was in 1833 superseded by the manufacture of the white and black silk guipures now so widely known as Maltese lace. This improvement was due to Lady Hamilton Chichester, who brought laceworkers over from Genoa to teach their craft in the island. Some of the patterns from that time showed the influence of the Genoese instruction. Maltese lace is made not only in Malta, but in Auvergne and Lepuy in France; in Buckinghamshire and Bedfordshire, in England, and also in the Irish lace schools. Ceylon and Madras lace also resembles Maltese. Formerly shawls and veils of much beauty and value were made of this lace, but the manufacture is now confined chiefly to narrow trimmings.

MECHLIN.—A pillow lace originally made at Mechlin, Belgium, and whose special characteristics are the narrow, flat thread, band or cord, which outlines the pattern, and the net ground of hexagonal mesh. Sometimes the mesh is circular. The net ground is made of two threads twisted twice on four sides and four threads plaited three times on the two other sides. In this it differs from Brussels lace, whose plait is longer and whose mesh is larger. The lace is made in one piece upon the pillow, the ground being formed with the pattern. The very finest thread is used, and a high degree of skill is necessary, so that the resulting fabric is very costly. It is a filmy, beautiful and highly transparent lace, and preserves for a very long time its distinguishing peculiarity of a shiny thread or band surrounding the outlines of the sprigs and dots of the design. The earliest Mechlin designs were very like those of Brussels lace, though not so original and graceful; but in this respect later Mechlin laces showed marked improvement. The funda-

Imitation Mechlin.

Imitation Torchon.

mental difference between the two, however, was that Mechlin was worked in one piece upon the pillow, while the Brussels pattern was first made by itself, and the réseau or net ground was afterward worked in around it. The manufacture of Mechlin has long been on the decline, the French Revolution seriously injuring the industry; and when the trade was revived and encouraged under Napoleon, the exquisite patterns of former times had been partly forgotten or were too expensive for popular demand. At the time of its highest popularity it was called the Queen of Laces, sharing that title with the finest Alençon point. Mechlin sometimes had an ornamental net ground called Fond du Neige, and also a ground of six-pointed Fond Champ, but these kinds were rare. It has always been a very great favorite with the English, and appears in most of their family collections of laces. There was a fine collection of this lace at the Paris Exhibition of 1867 from Turnhout, Belgium, as well as from other lace manufacturing centers.

MEDICI.—A name for a variety of modern torchon lace, whose distinguishing peculiarity is the insertion effect, the lace being very like an ordinary insertion, with the exception of having one edge finished with scallops. The Medici design is also characterized by plain, close-woven work, the close work alternating in equal amount with the open-work, the contrast between them heightening the effect.

MÉLANGE.—A heavy, black silk lace, distinguished by its mingling of Spanish patterns with ordinary Chantilly effects. The edge is usually plain and straight, but is sometimes ornamented with a fine silk fringe.

MIGNONETTE.—A light pillow lace, with an open ground resembling tulle, made in narrow strips. It was one of the earliest of pillow laces, and flourished greatly during the sixteenth, seventeenth and eighteenth centuries. It was made of Lille thread, and the chief places of its manufacture were Arras, Lille and Paris, in France, and in Switzerland.

MIRECOURT.—A lace made of detached sprigs upon a net made at the same time with the pattern. In the seventeenth century it was a French guipure lace of more delicate texture and varied design than other guipures. Mirecourt, in the Department of the Vosges, and its environs, were the center of the industry. The manufacture was begun at an early date, and for centuries only hempen thread was used, the result being a coarse guipure; but during the early part of the seventeenth century a finer lace of more delicate pattern was produced, and it began to be exported in considerable quantities. Before the union of Lorraine with France, in 1766, there was less than 800 laceworkers in Mirecourt, but in 1869 the number had increased to 25,000. During the last century the French demand for this lace increased far beyond the foreign demand, and it became desirable to produce a greater variety of pattern. This was done with great success by imitating the best designs. Another recent improvement at Mirecourt is the making of application flowers, and though these are not yet as finished as the Brussels sprigs, they bid fair to supply the French market, so as to make it to that extent independent of Belgium. The lace made at Mirecourt is mostly white. The work is similar in process and equal in quality to that of Lille and Arras.

NANDUTI.—A lace made by the natives of Paraguay, Ecuador and Peru, South America, from the soft, brilliant fiber of the agave plant. It is made in silk or thread by a needle on a cardboard pattern. In Peru and Ecuador it is also needle-made in the form of small squares and united together.

NEEDLE-POINT.—Real lace of any kind worked with a needle, on a parchment pattern, and not with bobbins or on a pillow. The distinction between needle-point and bobbin-made, or pillow lace, is also illustrated by the solid part of the pattern, and also the ground of the former. In needle-point the solid parts are invariably made of rows of buttonhole stitches, sometimes closely worked and sometimes with small open spaces left in the patterns. The "brides" in needle-point consist of one or two threads fastened across from one part of the pattern to another, and then closely buttonholed over; it will be found, also, that true needle-point is made with only one kind of stitch, the looped or buttonhole stitch already mentioned, and that this is constant amid all varieties of design in this kind of lace. Pillow lace, on the contrary, has a "toilé" made of threads crossing each other more or less at right angles; its "brides" consist of twisted or plaited threads, and the "picots" are simple loops, while the network ground of pillow lace is of far greater variety than that of needle-point. In all kinds of pillow lace the net groundwork is made by twisting and plaiting the threads, sometimes in twos and sometimes in fours. Briefly speaking, the fundamental difference between needle-point and pillow lace is that the former is made with looped stitches throughout, while the latter is made with twisted or plaited threads, which last is really weaving, though it is done with bobbins and the hand instead of with the loom.

ORIENTAL.—A lace made on the embroidering machine, which by combined needle and shuttle action produces either simple or complex designs upon netting. The action of the Schiffli machine somewhat resembles that of a sewing-machine, and the product is more properly called embroidery than lace. The openwork effects are produced either by the action of chemicals upon the foundation material, or by the use of the scissors. The threadwork results from the combined action of the shuttle and needles. St. Gall, Switzerland, and Plauen, Saxony, are the chief manufacturing centers for these laces, which include trimming and border laces, curtains, bed sets, shams, and the like. In the broad historical sense, Oriental laces and embroideries refer to the products of the East, especially to the Chinese, Indian, Japanese, Persian and Turkish. All these were remarkable for the labor expended upon

Real Renaissance.

Machine Valenciennes.

them, their great cost, and the originality and boldness of idea and coloring which marked their design.

OYAH.—A guipure lace or openwork embroidery, made by means of a hook in a fashion similar to crochet. The pattern is often elaborate, and in silks of many colors, representing flowers, foliage, etc. It is sometimes in relief.

PARCHMENT.—Lace in whose manufacture parchment has been used, whether in the pattern for the worker's guidance, or for stiffening the fabric, as in Cartisane lace. In old accounts of laces, the term was often applied to those made on the pillow to distinguish them from needle-point laces, and it was derived from the pattern on which pillow laces were worked.

PASSEMENT.—A term applied to the oldest class of pillow laces, at a time when they were of comparatively simple construction, being little more than open braids and gimps. This designation was in use until the middle of the seventeenth century. The word is now applied to a decorative edging or trimming, especially a gimp or braid. It is an old French word, and in the country of its origin included in its meaning both lace and embroideries. It has an interesting literary association, having figured, under the slightly altered form of "passemens," in a satirical poem published at Paris in 1661. The poem, which is entitled "La Révolte des Passemens," is dedicated to Mademoiselle de la Trousse, a cousin of Madame de Sévigné, and was probably composed by one of her literary friends. It is a protest against a sumptuary law passed in the previous year to check the lavish expenditure on laces imported from Venice and Italy, and is interesting as an account of the best laces of that day, among which are "Pointes de Gênes, de Raguse, de Venise, d'Angleterre et de Flanders," as well as the "Gueuse" of humbler pretensions. The various laces are supposed to revolt against the law excluding them from France, and especially from their

Imitation Point de Venise Combined with Point Gaze.

place in the exalted society of the court. Mesdames les Broderies—

> "Le Poincts, Dentelles, Passemens,
> Qui par une vaine despence,
> Ruinoient aujourd 'hui la France"—

call an indignation meeting. One of them hotly demands what punishment shall be meted out to the court for such treatment—

> "Dites moi je vous prie
> Poincts, dentelles ou broderies,
> Qu'aurons nous donc fait à la cour," etc.

Various laces speak their mind freely in reply, but most of them are gloomy as to the future, while a few try to take a philosophical view of the situation, and resign themselves to an humbler though still useful fate. An English lace, "une Grande Dentelle d'Angleterre" answers

> "Cet infortune sans seconde
> Elle fait bien renoncer au monde
> * * *
> Pour ne plus tourner à tout vent
> Comme d'entrer dans un Convent."

The laces of Flanders are not so submissive as that, being too vain and ambitious for renunciation of the world and life in a convent, and their angry opposition starts a little tempest of debate, fierce resolution alternating with despair. A black lace in hopeless mood hires herself out with a game merchant, for nets to catch snipe and woodcock. An old gold lace, in grandmotherly style, tries to comfort the younger ones, by reminding them of the vanity of the world. She knows all about it —she, who has dwelt in king's houses. The Flanders laces cry out that rather than give in they would sooner be sewn to the bottom of a petticoat. Some of the younger ones declare they must still have amusement, having had so much, and rather than renounce the world they will seek refuge in the masquerade shops. The point laces, with the exception of Aurillac, then resolve to go each to his own country, when suddenly the humble but plucky Gueuse lace, the lace of the common people, arrives from a village near Paris and encourages the others to fight it out.

The next morning they all assemble and agree upon a plan of campaign, but before doing so take stock of their qualifications and prospects. Poinct d'Alençon has a good opinion of herself; a Flanders lace says she made two campaigns under the king, as a cravat; another had been in the wars under the great Marshal Turenne; another was torn at the siege of Dunkirk; and all had done something worth notice. "What have we to fear?" asked an English lace. A Poinct de Génes, of rather flabby character, advises the English lace to go slow. Finally open war is declared, and the laces all assemble at the fair of St. Germain to be reviewed by General Luxe. The muster roll is called by Colonel Sotte Depense, and the various regiments and battalions march forth to victory or death. But they got neither, for at the first approach of the royal artillery they take to their heels, are captured and condemned to various punishments.

The gold and silver laces, the leaders of the rebellion, are sentenced to the fate of Jeanne D'Arc, to be burned alive; the points are condemned to be made into tinder for the sole use of the King's Musketeers; others are to be made into cordage or sent to the galleys. But pardon is obtained through the good offices of cunning little Cupid—"Le petit dieu plein de finesse," and the rebels are restored to their former position.

The poem illustrates the policy of most European governments at that time, a policy of excluding foreign manufactures of all kinds; and in the case of laces, the fear of encouraging wasteful habits among the rich, who offered a tempting opportunity for royal extortion, was too useful a pretence to be passed by. But all these efforts were fruitless to discourage the growth of lacemaking. The passion for beauty in personal adornment would not down. The engravings of Abraham Bosse, which portray the dress and manners of that time, humorously depict the despair of the fashionable lady over the prospect of giving up her laces. She is represented as attired in plain hemmed linen cuffs, collar and cap of Puritanical severity, bemoaning her sad fate, in heart-breaking strains, as she sorrowfully packs away her rich lace-trimmed costumes. Her sadness was not unduly prolonged. Colbert, the great French statesman, saw that laces would be smuggled if they were legally prohibited, that the rich would have them at any cost, so he encouraged foreign lacemakers to come to France, and the manufacture was thus promoted.

PILLOW.—Lace made on the pillow or cushion, both pattern and mesh being formed by hand. See Needle-point lace.

PLAITED.—A pillow lace of simple geometrical design, often made of strong and stiff strands, such as gold thread or fine braid. The pattern, besides being geometrical in design, is open, and has no grounds. For ordinary purposes tinsel is used instead of real gold, and the lace is then employed for theatrical purposes. Historically considered, the plaited laces made of gold, silver or silk thread, took the place of the Italian knotted laces of the sixteenth century. Those produced at Genoa and in Spain were the best, and they are made in Spain to-day, chiefly for church uses. The thread plaited laces of the seventeenth century were used to trim ruffs and falling collars, but went out of fashion when flowing wigs came in, as the latter hid the collar and would not allow ruffs to be worn. At the present time plaited laces have become known under the name of Maltese and Cluny, and are made at Auvergne, in France, Malta, and in the English counties of Bedfordshire and Buckinghamshire.

Real Maltese.

Real Guipure.

PLAUEN.—A name applied to any kind of lace made at Plauen, Saxony, or elsewhere, upon the embroidering machine, such as Oriental, tulle and chiffon lace, Point de Venise, Point d'Irlande. Plauen led in the manufacture of this kind of lace, having begun it in 1881, from which year dates the importance of that city as a lace market. The manufacture was gradually developed. Only the tulle variety of embroidery lace was produced until 1886. The distinguishing feature of this was that the hollow effects were made by opening the tulle meshes by hand. Then, in 1886, an openwork process was invented by which chemical action was employed to remove a woolen or silk foundation from the cotton-embroidered pattern, or a cotton foundation from a silk embroidery that had been worked on it. This made it possible to form the pattern by the embroidery machine in the same way as in the case of ordinary embroidery. The wool foundation, which is necessary to be removed in finishing the goods, is dissolved by the action of certain chemicals without changing the cotton or silk pattern. In this way the most difficult and complicated patterns of real lace can be imitated. Plauen manufacturers have for the most part taken the old and costly hand-made laces of former times for their models; but they have also originated new and tasteful designs from time to time.

POINT APPLIQUÉ.—Point lace whose design is separate from the net ground, to which it is afterward applied. At the present time the net ground is usually machine-made. The word "point," however, in this connection, is of variable application, sometimes signifying Point Appliqué, and sometimes denoting lace, whether pillow or needle-point; that is, worked in sprays and laid upon a machine-net ground. (See Application lace.)

POINT D'ALENÇON.—See Alençon.

POINT D'ANGLETERRE.—See English Point.

POINT DE GAZE.—A very fine, gauze-like lace, made entirely with the needle and grounded with its own net. Point de Gaze is the result of an attempt of the Brussels lacemakers to return to the best early traditions of needle-point. Point de Gaze differs, however, from the finest old needle-point in certain respects, partly necessitated by modern taste in design, and partly from the need of great economy in labor costs. For example, the execution is much more open and delicate than in the early lace of this description, but this very delicacy and slightness are made use of to produce a very elegant effect. Part of the toile, or substance of the pattern, is made in close and part in open stitch, giving an appearance of shading, and the open parts are very tastefully ornamented with dots. The result does not in all respects equal the softness and richness of the early lace, but if Point de Gaze seems thin and loose in comparison, and if the patterns seem less ideally beautiful, nevertheless the later work has a unique lightness and delicacy to which the earlier lace did not attain. It certainly is the most etherial and delicately beautiful of all point laces. Its forms are not emphasized by a raise outline of buttonhole stitching, as in Point d'Alençon and Point d'Argentan, but are simply outlined by a thread.

POINT DE GÈNE.—A name at present applied to a species of lace made both in cotton and silk at St. Gall and Plauen, and recognized by its regular net ground and large, open patterns in heavy stitchwork. It is a popular trimming for women's dresses. Point de Gène, or Gènes, was originally one of the laces made at the city of Genoa and in the surrounding country during the seventeenth century, both the pillow and needle laces made there being deservedly famous. Gold and silver thread and gold wire were used in the manufacture of the earliest needle-point laces at Genoa, and the gold wire was drawn out in exact imitation of the early Greek method. One of the best Genoese laces resembles the early Greek points in patterns. There was also a guipure lace, made from aloe fiber, as well as the knotted lace now known as Macramé. The last named is the only lace at present made in Genoa, and along the seacoast.

PoInt d'Esprit.—A term applied to a small oval or square figure, peculiar to certain varieties of early guipure, and ordinarily composed of three short lengths of parchment or cord, placed side by side and covered with thread. These oval or square figures were most commonly arranged in the form of rosettes. At present the term Point d'Esprit denotes a much smaller solid or mat surface, used to diversify the net ground of some laces. It is in the form of small squares that set at close and regular intervals. In standard histories of lace the term is also used as synonymous with embroidered tulle, made in Brittany, Denmark and around Genoa.

Point d'Irlande.—A coarse, machine-made imitation of real Venetian point lace. It is popular for dress trimmings, and is manufactured in a great variety of widths in cotton and silk. It has no net ground, the patterns being united by brides.

Point de Milan.—A guipure lace with a small mesh ground, and the pattern distinguished by striking scroll designs. The flowers in the pattern of hand-made Point de Milan are flat, and have the appearance of having been wrought in close-woven linen. Milan point was made at the city of that name in 1493. Gold and silver thread were first used, but the Milan points were finer than these, and fully equal to the best Spanish and Venetian points.

Point de Paris.—Originally a narrow pillow lace, resembling Brussels. The term is now generally applied to a machine-made cotton lace of simple pattern and inferior quality. In its making a design whose figures, such as flowers and leaves, are outlined with a heavy thread, is worked upon a net ground. Point de Paris is distinguished by the net, which is hexagonal in form.

Point de Venise.—See Venice Point.

Imitation Irish Crochet.

Point.—Same as Needle-point lace, made wholly by hand, with the needle and a single thread.

Pot.—Lace whose pattern is distinguished by the figure of a vase or deep dish, and sometimes by that of a basket containing flowers. It is the best-known lace made at Antwerp, and was formerly in common use in that city for decorating women's caps. The vase and basket figures vary much in size and design. Some have considered this pattern to be a survival from an earlier design, including the figure of the Virgin and the Annunciation, but this is not certain.

Powdered.—Lace whose ground is strewn with small, separate ornaments, such as flowers, sprigs, or squares, like Point d'Esprit. The term is applied also to whitened lace.

Renaissance.—A modern point lace, whose patterns are made of narrow braid, and united by bars or filling of different kinds. It is generally ornamented with circular figures and scroll-work, stitched in place by needle and thread, the intervening spaces or groundwork, being composed of a variety of fancy openwork. Irish Renaissance, Luxeuil and Battenberg are the other names for this lace.

Rose Point.—See Venice Point.

Saxony.—Fine drawnwork embroidered with the needle, in much demand in the eighteenth century. At the present time the term is somewhat vague, denoting many kinds of laces made in Saxony, especially in imitation of old Brussels lace. Though the latter is the best that is made, a coarse guipure lace, known as Etervelle, and plaited lace has the greatest sale.

Rose Point.—See Venice Point.

Seaming.—A narrow openwork insertion, gimp or braiding, with parallel sides, used for joining two breadths of linen, instead of sewing them directly the one to the other. The name is given to a similar lace used for edgings, as in the trimming of pillow-cases and sheets. During the sixteenth and seventeenth centuries this lace was very popular, though the name "seaming" was then applied to any kind of lace used for a particular purpose—namely, to insert in the linen or other fabric wherever a seam appeared, and often where no seam was really necessary. The lace first used for this purpose was cut-work; then Hollie point became fashionable, and afterward the custom grew to be so common that cheaper laces were employed. There is still in existence a sheet decorated with cut-work that once belonged to Shakespeare.

SILVER.—A passement or guipure wholly or in large part composed of silver wire, or of warp threads of silk, or silk and cotton combined, wound with a thin, flat ribbon of silver. See Gold lace.

SPANISH.—A general term applies to the following four different kinds of lace: (a) Needle-point lace, brought from Spanish convents after their dissolution, though the art of making it is thought by some to have been learned in Flanders. (b) Cut and drawnwork made in Spanish convents, of patterns usually confined to simple sprigs and flowers. (c) A modern black silk lace with large flower patterns. (d) A modern needle-made fabric, the pattern usually in large squares. The machine-made black and white silk laces, with their flower patterns, are from Lyons and Calais, France. Much could be said about the uncertain application of the term "Spanish" in regard to certain kinds of lace. It has often been inaccurately used. For instance, "Spanish Point" and "Point d'Espagne" have been misapplied to Italian laces, in the same way that "Point d'Angleterre" has been misapplied to Brussels lace. In the four kinds of Spanish lace above enumerated, it is noticeable that some are of Flemish origin. A lace known for certain to be of Spanish origin is a coarse pillow guipure made in white thread and also of gold and silver. It is a loosely made fabric consisting of three cordonnets, the center one being the coarsest, united by finer threads running in and out across them, and with brides to join the parts of the pattern and keep them in shape. It is well known that large quantities of lace that have the characteristics of raised Venetian Point were used in Spain, both for court dresses and church purposes, such as the ornamentation of vestments and altars. During the invasion of Napoleon the churches and monasteries were pillaged and the laces contained therein were scattered abroad and sold as being of Spanish origin, though many of them were not.

The graceful Spanish headdress, the mantilla, has been chiefly made in the province of Catalonia, out of black and white Blondes, but it is inferior to a similar lace of French manufacture. The most celebrated of the Spanish laces are the gold and silver fabrics, known as Point d'Espagne, the Blonde laces and Spanish or Rose point. The first-named is a very old lace, was known in Spain as early as the middle of the fifteenth century, and is made with gold and silver threads, upon which a pattern is embroidered in colored silk. The Blondes, which have been already mentioned, have thick though graceful patterns upon a light net ground. Rose point is wholly made with the needle and is very like Venetian point, being considered, in fact, as a variety of the latter. The close resemblance is accounted for by the fact that this kind of lace was made by the inmates of religious houses, which were transferred from one country to another at the will of their superior and carried with them the secret of a difficult art. The Rose points, some of which are not raised, are formed with a pattern-worked net in buttonhole stitches, the parts of the pattern being joined together by brides. The raised Rose points are recognized by their thick cordonnet or outlining of the pattern.

TAMBOUR.—Lace made with needle embroidery upon a machine-made net, generally black or white Nottingham. It is chiefly made in Ireland and commonly included among the Limerick laces.

TAPE.—A lace made with the needle, except that a tape or narrow

Leavers's Lace Machine.

strip of linen is wrought into the work and is the distinguishing feature of the pattern. These plain or ornamented tapes or braids, arranged so as to form the pattern, have always been peculiar to this kind of lace. The patterns are connected together with either bride or net grounds. The earliest were made with a bride ground and simple cloth stitch, but gradually very elaborate designs were wrought as part of the braid-like patterns and united by open-meshed grounds. In the seventeenth and eighteenth centuries the braid and tape laces included the large majority of coarse pillow laces made in Flanders, Spain and Italy.

THREAD.—Lace made from linen thread as distinguished from silk and cotton laces. Black thread is a misnomer for Chantilly.

TORCHON.—A coarse pillow lace made of strong, soft and loosely twisted thread. In Europe it is known also as "Beggars'" lace, and the old French Gueuse lace was similar to Torchon. The patterns generally are very simple and formed with a loose stout thread and the ground is coarse net. Torchon is now also machine made.

VALENCIENNES.—A solid and durable pillow lace having the same kind of thread throughout for both ground and pattern. Both the pattern and ground are wrought together by the same hand, and as this demands much skill in the manipulation of a great many threads and bobbins, the price of Valenciennes is very high. The mesh of the ground is usually square or diamond shaped, very open and of great regularity. It is a flat lace, worked in one piece, and no different kind of thread is introduced to outline the pattern or to be wrought into any part of the fabric. This affords a ready means of distinguishing the hand-made variety of this lace. The Valenciennes now made is not so beautiful in design and construction as the fabric of an earlier date, especially in the latter part of the eighteenth century. It is usually of narrower width and is easier to learn how to make.

Valenciennes was first made at the town of that name, which, though originally Flemish, was transferred to France by treaty; and the manufacture at this town was carried on under conditions which assured the superiority of the lace produced there. The difference between the Valenciennes product and that of other towns could be detected by the softer "feel" in the former case, because the moist climate of Valenciennes gave a smoother action to the bobbins when used in manufacture; and it is interesting to note that the lace was made in underground rooms. These peculiarities earned for lace made in that town the name of Vraie Valenciennes, and it brought a higher price than the Valenciennes of the surrounding villages. The thread was spun from the finest flax. To buy a yard of a flounce or a pair of broad ruffles was a serious matter for the purchaser unless he was wealthy. The labor cost was high even in those days of low wages; from 300 to 1,200 bobbins were required in a piece of fine work. The history of the changes in Valenciennes patterns is, to some extent, a history of deterioration in elegance of design. The first patterns were exquisitely beautiful, the designs often being wrought in grounds that were varied in several ways even in one piece. The designs afterward became simpler, and octagon and hexagon meshes came to take the place of the close grounds of earlier manufacture. Since 1780 the lighter and less expensive laces of Lille, Brussels and Arras have partly ousted the more beautiful, costly and durable product of Valenciennes, while changes in modern dress have stopped the demand for some articles which were formerly among the fashionable mainstays of the industry; for example, men's ruffles.

The French Revolution practically destroyed lacemaking at Valenciennes, and the industry was transferred to Belgium. The lace produced there was, however, given the name of False Valenciennes. Alost, Bruges, Ypres, Ghent, Menin and Courtrai became centers of the manufacture, and the lace made in each town had a distinguishing feature in the ground. For example, the Ghent ground is square meshed, the bobbin being twisted two and one-half times. At Ypres, the ground is square meshed, but the bobbins are twisted four times. In Courtrai and Menin, the bobbins are twisted three and a half times, and in Bruges three times. As an illustration of the fact that the making of old Valenciennes is a lost art, it is interesting to note that the last important piece of work executed within that town was a headdress presented by the town to the Duchesse de Nemoms on her marriage in 1840. The headdress was made by old women, the few real Valenciennes laceworkers then surviving, with the praiseworthy and patriotic object of showing the perfection of the product of former days. There are several machine-made varieties of Valenciennes. English Valenciennes is chiefly made at Nottingham; it is also called Platt and Normandy Valenciennes. It is an imitation of the early hand-made lace, to the extent of having a similar diamond-meshed ground. Its pattern is without relief, and the threads of which it is made are no heavier than the ground. French Valenciennes is made mostly at Calais. Its pattern is usually outlined by a stouter thread than that forming the ground, and it has a finer finish and softer "feel" than the English Valenciennes; in fact, it is an excellent imitation of the real. Italian Valenciennes is a narrow, fine-threaded lace, used for trimming fine underwear.

VENICE POINT.—A needle-point lace made at Venice during the first half of the seventeenth century. It is somewhat difficult to apply the name exclusively to any one of the several varieties of Venetian point made at that time; but Venetian Raised point, whose pattern is of large, beautifully designed flowers in decided relief and united by brides or bars, is commonly called Venetian point. Other names applied to this kind of lace are Rose point, Venetian Flat point, Carnival lace, Cardinal's point, Pope's point, and Point d'Espagne. These names simply register the various changes of style and manufacture in the history of

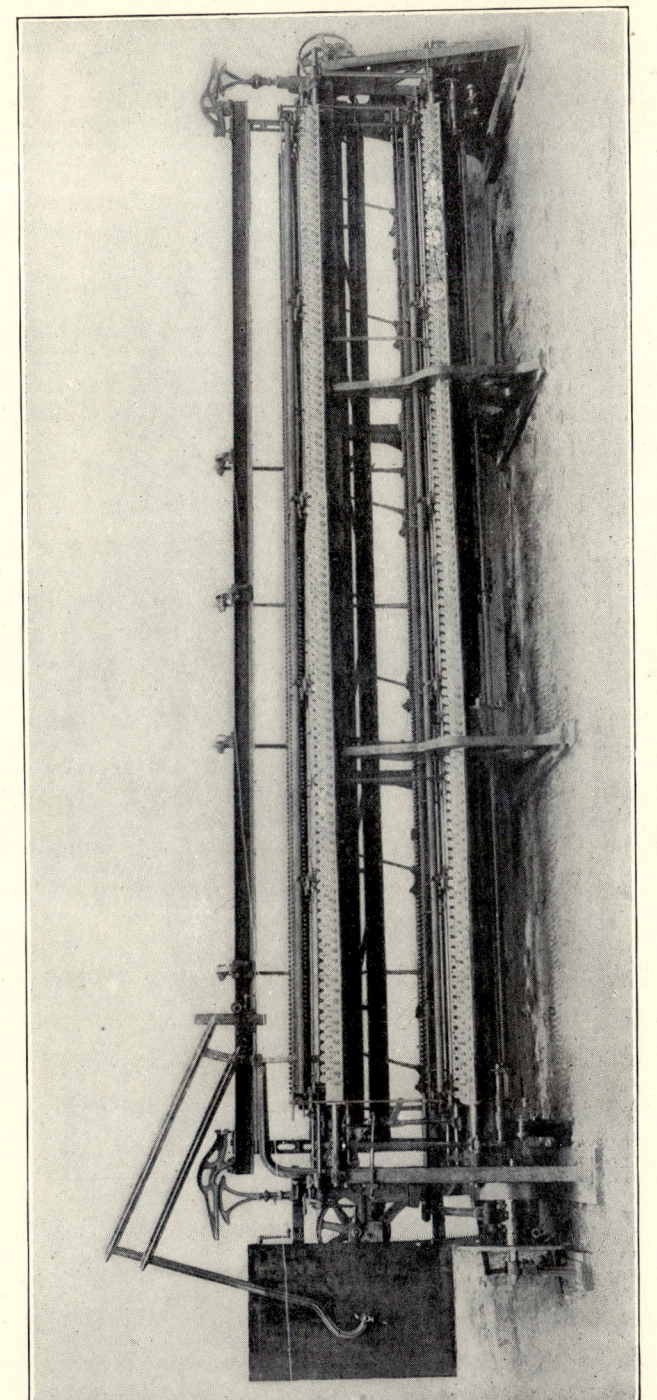

Schiffli or Power Embroidering Machine.

this lace. With the exception of Point d'Espagne, which has a less valid claim to be called Venetian point than the others, the various names given serve roughly to suggest the distinction between three separate stages in point of style and date of the fabric known broadly as "Punto tagliato a foliani," or Venetian point. They are generally given as follows: (1) Venetian Raised point, or Gros Point de Venise, under which is included Rose point; (2) Venetian Flat point, or Point Plat de Venise, with its later variety, known as Coraline point; (3) Grounded Venetian point, or Point de Venise à Réseau, which includes Burano point, so called from the island near Venice, where it was made. With regard to Raised point, it is worth noting, in addition to the characteristics already referred to, that the flower design is of a freedom and continuity that make the pattern so filling that there is very little space left for the ground, the bridework merely serving to hold the pattern strongly together. The cordonnet, or outlining thread, is unusually prominent, and the raised part is no less remarkable for its boldness in design than for its delicate workmanship. An Italian poet has described this work as "sculptured in relief." In Raised point the skill of the lace-worker was informed by the instinct for beauty in such a degree as to produce one of the highest types of the art. Rose point resembles Raised point in all essential features, the only difference being that the designs are smaller and the ornamentation more abundant. The pattern is less filling and the connecting brides more prominent.

Flat Venetian point is marked by an absence of the prominent raised work, the designs are more attenuated, and the brides are altogether more prominent than in the Raised point. Coraline point is a variety of Flat point, which must be considered a deterioration in design on account of its ill-connected and irregular pattern, which was originally supposed to imitate a branch of coral. There is no raised work, the ground meshes are ill-arranged and ill-shaped, and on the whole this lace marks the decadence of an art formerly almost perfect. It is more like an imitation of a free growth of plants, the tangled growth of a state of nature, as compared with the order and beauty of art. The grounded point, the last stage of development of Venetian lace, began to be made to supply the markets of France after the fine old Venetian point had been excluded by protective laws. The Venetian lacemakers then adopted the réseau or net ground made at Alençon. The ground is composed of double twisted threads, and has a rounder mesh than Alençon, and there is no outlining cordonnet. In this variety of Venetian point, which was produced during the latter half of the eighteenth century, the pattern is not so well arranged as in others, and there is a redundancy of ornamentation. The manufacture of Venetian point is now almost extinct. The machine-made variety, produced on the Schiffli embroidery frame, is now made at Plauen and St. Gall. (See Plauen lace.)

YAK.—A stout, coarse pillow lace, made from the fine wool of the Yak. The patterns are of simple, geometrical design, connected with plaited guipure bars that form part of the pattern, being made out of the same threads at the same time. The term is also applied to a machine-made worsted lace, produced in black, white and colors. It is used as a trimming for undergarments, shawls and petticoats.

YPRES.—A pillow lace resembling Valenciennes, but sometimes with bolder designs and rather large lozenge or square mesh in the ground; also a type of Valenciennes.

R
746
g G61
c.1

**PLEASE USE IN
LIBRARY ONLY**